Jane Lovell

The God of Lost Ways

Indigo Dreams Publishing

First Edition: The God of Lost Ways
First published in Great Britain in 2020 by:
Indigo Dreams Publishing
24, Forest Houses
Cookworthy Moor
Halwill
Beaworthy
Devon
EX21 5UU

www.indigodreams.co.uk

Jane Lovell has asserted her right under the Copyright, Designs
and Patents Act 1988 to be identified as the author of this work.
© Jane Lovell 2020

ISBN 978-1-912876-41-9

British Library Cataloguing in Publication Data. A CIP record
for this book can be obtained from the British Library.

Designed and typeset in Palatino Linotype by Indigo Dreams.
Cover image: *Goldleaf: a John Atkinson Grimshaw homage*
© Saffron Swansborough
Printed and bound in Great Britain by 4edge Ltd.

Papers used by Indigo Dreams are recyclable products made
from wood grown in sustainable forests following the guidance
of the Forest Stewardship Council.

For remembered days of Erw Wen,
La Jardière and the Greensand Way

Acknowledgements

Poems in this collection have previously appeared in Agenda, American Journal of Poetry, Dark Mountain, Elementum Journal, Finished Creatures, Live Encounters, Mslexia, New Welsh Review, Poetry News, Poetry Wales, Riggwelter, The Curlew, The High Window, The Interpreter's House, The Lonely Crowd, The Poetry Shed, Wild Court and Zoomorphic, and in the anthologies 'For the Silent' (IDP 2019) and Pale Fire (Frogmore Press 2019).

'Equivocal' won the Flambard Prize in 2015.
'Milk' was shortlisted for the Basil Bunting Prize in 2016.

In 2018, 'Starlings' won the Wigtown Poetry Competition and 'Orchards, Greensand Way' won the Wealden Literary Festival Writing Competition.
'Night Fox with Stars' was runner-up in the 2019 Ambit Poetry Competition.

Also by Jane Lovell

Metastatic (Against the Grain Poetry Press, 2018)
One Tree (Night River Wood, 2018)
Forbidden (Coast to Coast to Coast, 2019)
This Tilting Earth (Seren, 2019)

CONTENTS

The God of Lost Ways

The God of Lost Ways

Phantom, mercurial,
he follows cracks in pavements,
the upside curve of bridges,
the outer edge of lamplight,

in your darkest moments
brings you blown trees with shards
of pottery and coins in their roots,
skeletons of fry in the carcass of a fish,
seedpods in rasping spirals.

He is a night-bird folded on the fencepost
counting ten for the mice to run
or a motorway hoverer
hypnotised by the jiggery of voles
in the buffeted grass.

When you are drowning in the enormity
of days,
he offers you sea glass, the shiver
of dune grass, an eel switching
across slipstreams of mud.

He unfurls new leaves
to patch holes in your skies,
linnets and pipits to stitch paths
across your discarded landscapes.

He is that jay's feather in your hand,
the bird's egg of flint, its cracked black seams,

and that greenlip marble you found in landslip
that took you all the way back
to the start.

Plum

The wild plum, uprooted and filling
the garden with leaf and greenlight,
offends you. It does not die
but sends out the most delicate of shoots.
I cover its roots with damp soil, support
its trunk with a spade and the prop
from the clothes' line.

You need your trees to be vertical.
It knows your frustration and continues
to grow undeterred, quietly collecting
birdsong in its phloem,
tucking it away in bright sharp notes.
It stores breezes in its leaves for still days,
rain in its roots for dry days,
holds in its heartwood the blessing
of patience.

In its cave I am held safe and invisible.
My whole world is green.
I am absorbed into the planet's breathing.
I hide below, beckon you in.

Hare

Early morning air
slice-cold below total blue
and he's sitting bold as a stray on the lawn,
tasting the breeze, absorbing every ripple
with those planetary ears.

Time passes only in the shiver of leaves,
a solitary beetle ticking in the sage.

In a heartbeat, he's away to the skyline,
unzipping the grass and wind-chased verge,
giving us the whole month of May
stretched languorously through centuries,
myrtle, mint and purple betony,
twirling her skirts,
shaking her hair in the wind,

gathering speed as if in huntdown,
as if pinning the lawn with his longbone feet,
bursting through streamers of birdsong,
scattering like confetti the trimmings
of finch and sparrow,
carrying his ears so beautifully,
so beautifully,
all the way to the furthest corner

where he pauses,
resting on his haunches
in the lee of a budding lilac
and breathes,
breathes the whole sky:
invisible worlds,
distant constellations,
pared-down moon.

Margaret

Your garden thrives in neglect.
The peony has never looked so good, so vibrant;
her blooms loll like woozy ladies on a lawn
brilliant with lipstick and scandal.

Finches steal discarded cocktail sticks,
appear on the wire, beaks stumped with olives.
Blackbirds stitch a path into the bushes
clutching bright worms of pimento.

Dandelions secure the lawn,
stop it flapping to reveal the wool
of root fibre, scurrying ants.

You left this afternoon, wrapped in blankets.
The rooms next door buzzed briefly then fell silent.

Within the hour, bedclothes appeared on the line,
caught the May wind in a flurry of lemon and lace,
waved you a final goodbye.

Blackbird

A conduit from sky to earth
he holds the perfect angle,

steals into his keyhole portal
bird-shaped pieces of anti-matter.

Planets course through,
constellations, that black stuff
that surrounds stars and goes on forever.

He tilts his beak – a final swish of laurel,
softwood echoes for his evening song –

then trucks along on twiggy legs
delicate and tough as hazel.

He owns this:
day, space, runway of path and lawn.

He is his own person: dark thief, shaman,
practising the old ways of the ouzel,

stores storm and midnight in his feathers,
hops them into drifts of dry leaves,

seduces worms with his rain dance,
stamps them up from secret crumbling halls,

holds them twisting and curling
in his tight yellow beak,

the globe of his eye capturing the whole world
and you
in a quiet blink.

Funeral for an Owl

The smoke betrays you, balling out into the room
to hang like a shroud.

Stopped in the flue above the baffle, wings folded
at terrible angles, there is nothing to you

but a beautiful, plumed husk, light as a wasps' nest,
woven from the thinnest bones.

Outside, a gusting breeze seeks to resurrect you.
We dream your damson heart quickens

at the scurried grass, its possibilities of mice and shrew,
but you are long gone,

deceived by the darkness that shielded you,
the black promise that drew you in.

As the May sun chases shadows across the ground,
to the song of blackcap and wren we carry you

to the far field, its riven oak swarming with ivy,
and prop you inside the trunk: a ball of soft nothing,

one small hole that remembers your eye
and claws gnarled knots that could only scratch and scuff

the dreadful steel, your last glare fixed
on the far circle of stars above your twisted wing.

Two men and a hornets' nest

Two men and a hornets' nest on a day
whipped with leaves: the hornets' nest high
out of reach in the chimney stack, its smoke
wandering out to be blown to hell
over a moonscape of scattered foam,

and the men, thin and skanked, drawn down
to skin and bone by a lowlit world,
an underworld, bones defining nettled skin
in some determined way as if to hold their own
against the light.

Oh, the hoot they'd had, like some circus act,
balancing their makeshift pole rigged
with wire and canisters of gas, wheeling
twenty, thirty foot up, aiming the jet at a crack
in the brick.

We pass round the binoculars and chat.
Our new neighbours tell us they are Christians:
they don't drink; they are clean. It's been hard,
too complicated to explain, but they're here now
and it's OK.

They're the lucky ones, they say,
watching the crack, its pudding of bright foam,
and the last few hornets clunking drunkenly
at the stack, butting and looping back and fore
in the bewildered air.

The Longest Day

In the picture is a man below a creaking bough
in shades of green, a blotch of purple where a shadow
has been caught.
Short drop: skin-snag,
no ruck of bone against the strain.

It is the longest day; the sun has sharpened all the grass,
a dragonfly that weaves its mesmerising blue in time-lapse
flight above the pond,
the chair beneath the tree along which crawls a nodding wasp.
It took longer than you thought, this way.

It is the longest day, and soon your father will be home.
A combine grinds through fields, unflinching midday light.
Kites turn upon their wingtips at the suddenness of mice,
glide low like *Barcud Coch*
stitched tight inside his cabinet of glass.

It is the longest day: June 1993.
Elder drips its fruit upon the road, the lime kilns fill
with creeping buttercup and dock.
A twisted cat, railing at the wire embedded in its hip,
falls silent in the copse

and Don is home and running from his car across the grass.
Insects wind into the sky, a crane fly struggles in the pond.
The air is ocean-deep; it beaches him beneath the tree.
I see him wrap his arms around your legs
and weep.

The wings kill me

The wings kill me,
folded like that
as if to fend off light,

his skull between my fingers
– *a blackcap's pale egg* –
such a fragile thing,
its smudged pigment
            calcite bloom.

Once he was all beak
            and desperate,
soft as soot, soft as the dark.

Now, legs snapped stalks,
his whole being is papered in
and balanced on its keel,
            ribs a coracle
floundering in a sea
of black space.

Above him
lost days tilt bright and
            unreachable
at the chimney's edge.

Oh the song he'll never sing,
the softest song held like a prayer
in his silent form.

Cimitero di Santa Maria

Beyond the wild gardens
and tumbled walls of Via dei Spironi,
a hidden graveyard for dogs
and seagulls unveils its bones:

atrophied remains of *levrieri*,
crouching *volpini*, folded carcasses
of gulls from St. Elena, wings stripped
to stalks, the eggshell skulls.

There are shells strung from trees,
an early sun and mist rising
from the tousled grass, rosettes
of lichen in pits of weathered stone.

The light is blown-glass, sea-rinsed
opal, scattered.
You can taste the salt in the air.

When no one is watching, shadows
chase the paths and soar across
the belfry; skinny cats jink through
on a breeze and a prayer.

It cannot last; the seas are rising.
Our city is a fortress
but the Earth is drowning;

the monastery, its fractured walls
festooned with cinquefoil, ivy,
flaked with *cocci* dug from shores
of mud and sand, is sinking.

Listen to the angels' watery voices.
Listen to the trickling of water
lifting the bones.

On Rye Hill

We make our nests in the ribs and skulls
of the blessed, blunt claws scuffing root and soil
from earthy chambers, their rafters of bone.

Evenings, we scatter from the scent of fox
and footfall, stretch into shadow below bramble,
remote stones resting in low sun.

We listen to the leaves and the wind
and the silence of the fox, the babble
of finches flitting to firs from plumes of salvia.

Time passes in the creep of ivy through
the ruined chapel, in songs diminishing
through planes of waves and sky.

We come and go. There are no ghosts here.
No one tends the dead.
No flowers decay in jars of rain.

We come and go,
our days measured by the tilting of the light
and the bloom of the grass
while the sea below beats like a great heart.

Something about Lily

There's something about walking these streets
with a dog.
There's something about passing through
the clamour of voices, past bars and market stalls,
bright fruits adrift with wasps,
with a dog held loosely on a loop of rope
that pads along beside you as if nothing is amiss,
joining you to the earth, the rock below, the planet,
as if you grew here, like a tree.

Bougainvillea, creeping passionflower, lilies in pots,
the sea beyond the leaning pines.
She trots beside you, a picture of nonchalance
and, for a while, allows you to forget that image
of torn haunch, skin lapped back to a mess
of muscle and the thin curl like a tiny moon
which might be bone.

Bougainvillea, creeping passionflower, lilies in pots,
doorways stacked with cheeses and oils.
The rope is loose and people greet her, *Leely Leely,*
and she is all wag and foxy; her eyes brimming longing.
She wiggles a bit, that damaged hip. A lop-sided wag.
It comes back to you sometimes: the heaving chest
and far off look. She didn't know you,
didn't understand the tarmac and its black stink.

Leely, Leely. She wanders along beside you, this dog,
past the grappa man with his scraps of ham,
the girl with kind hands who sells linens and tat.
There's something about walking these streets
with a dog, those glances she gives you.
There's something about her.

Orchards, Greensand Way

We meet between converging lines:
branch, twig, leaf, the bulbous fruit,
knuckles of root in ribbled ground

hands that led the plough, that hauled
and dug and cropped, *cup and twist*,
and gone. Those days like leaves.

Flagged tracks wind in from lanes
conjuring the old ways, trundle and scrape
of wheels through ghosts of trees.

The sun is brighter now, a black macramé
of tubes irrigates the lines; tractors grind
through vineyards on the south slopes.

We spot fox trails, vertical earth below
skylit hedges; from the ridge, every shade
of green laid out across the Weald, sweeping

to the mauve horizon of a wide unhurried sky.
Windfalls scatter the path: Cox's and crabs,
in the hedges, late bramble, damson,

each bite of fruit surprising in its freshness,
its poignancy.

Erw Wen

In the dim kitchen
your fingers knead and pull the dough,
flour smudges the yellow light
of your cheek and chin.
Poppy seeds escape across the table
disappear onto the tiles.

Red-eyed herring sprawl on the drainer,
flat and finless, silver.
The knife slits, scrapes out strings
and slips of skin;
worm-tangle on quaggy newsprint.

Liquor of fruit broods over must.
Bruised pulp smears the neck
plugged to protect
from the last vinegar flies
fat and desperate with eggs.

Oven hums, yeast creams in a jar.
You measure sugar, boil water.
I kneel to mash the blackberries.
Juice stains my fingers, blackens
my nails,

the sweetness bewildering
against hot bread.

Hallowe'en Cat

Twelve moons
since the blackslam collision
of stars and tarmac,
the bloodbang in her tiny head,
breath creeping out and away
from the streetlight blare,

we still expect
her raven howl on the stair,
her softpaw tread across pillows,
a gentle weight settling between us
like snow.

October ends, cloudless and cold.
Across a deepening sky she stretches,
the tip of each claw embedded
and gleaming.

She shimmers in snailscript,
the lucent geometry of spiders,
timmering leaftip dew.

The curve of her back amazes my hand:
she defines the space that is below her,
that is no longer tangible;
a place of black light,
the hallowed sky.

She is still here.

Her image ghosts the night
like unexpected frost.

She is the intake of breath when
headlights slice shadows,
when the world stops

and something running
catches your eye.

Night Fox with Stars

You did not expect her, so brazen,
dragging your dreams from their moorings
with her fishwife scold.

Eerie as seafog, and as wisp, she weaves
her spell, alert to every whit and scrattle
of leaf, rat or shrew.

Look how she holds her head just above
the surface of the night, breathes
the dead light of stars,

breathes the day's footsteps,
reads the scents and shadows, conjures
in her mind's eye:

the girls who waft their soaps and smoke
outside the salon on the corner;

the builder kneeling on the flags,
his fume of bitumen on lead;

the schoolboys hurling rotting pears
and quinces in the alley;

the man who heaves his crippled dog
outside to piss;

and the one who does not dream
but watches in the darkness as she passes
like a spectre,

her tin-screech bark scraping
all the stars and planets from their fixings,
summoning the daemons,

unsettling the oceans, jarring every nerve
along the knuckled backbone
of the night.

He loves her, this wild thing that steals away
his hours, leaves him wondering
at the solitude of stars.

The Tamworth Three

Stuffed like old sofas, they plough relentlessly
the wet soil, its slate-cold tang of Greensand spring,
truffling up roots and insects, worms.

Mornings, we see them joined in one great doughy heap
in their corrugated hut, bloating gently in frostlight
till the sun ripens their skin.

They know us. They watch us climb the length
of Beggars Lane and run to meet us,
ears flapping as they barrel to the fence,
their vintage violin-edged bellows-grunt greeting us
across the fractured land.

We name them:

Cindy, the fat one who lets herself out to forage
for acorns, chuntering and crunching in and out
of driveways, giving you the nod as you drag
your bewildered dog along the road;

Doreen the dwarf, with her high heels
and shit-slapped legs, rooting in ruts of mud,
circus-act pig with her strutting and somersaults
for the fencepost crows;

and the mean one, bullygirl Curly,
her jealous squinty eyes and crossbreed blackspot hide,
standing her ground in the foothills
of stinking straw.

We see them each day, until a wind-whipped
rain-blown morning just before Christmas

when, suddenly and eerily, their pen is empty:
a harsh mud-squish emptiness,
a rain-filled hoof-stippled Somme of silence.

We turn east to walk the edges of the orchards,
the last few apples red baubles in dripping rows
of wind-stripped trees

and squadrons of fieldfares
chortling and cackling in the high beeches
at so many windfalls, such a feast.

Pheasant

He will not blend with stone,
displays himself resolutely,
buffeted as he is, tousled
and leaf-bombed by gales
of passing traffic,

one glazed eye
in that perfectly-combed brow
oblivious to the broken
terracotta, charcoal,
bone of him

and the spindles of his wings
opening and closing
as if some strange semaphore
could summon the gods
to resurrect him.

Magpie

One for the belly, soft as an eye,
Two for a tongue and a beak stretched wide,
Three for a feather adrift in the sky,

Four for an egg and five for the yolk,
Six for the pulse of an embryo,
Seven for a fledgling when the mother has flown,

Eight for an eye, a lamb in the snow,
Nine for the scream of a crouching toad,
Ten for the grume of fox on the road.

Spit three times and say good day,
Raise your hat and I'll fly away.
Take no note and risk my curse:
You'll wake up deep in the grizzled earth.

Devil, I defy thee?
Devil may care!
I'll build my nest from your bones and hair.
One-two-three-four-FLY!

Kestrel hunting, East Sutton Churchyard

So sweet the mice; beak snips
through bones of whispered prayer,
        bellies stuffed with moss.

Born in the tight wool of prayer mats,
curled in a heaving knot, crumpled
and hairless, scrotal,
                        they know only
warmth,
the flutter of their mother's caged heart.

In time, eyes open, sharpen; they grow
to love the half-light,
                        its sheltered shadows,
venture out into furrows between
        lichened stone,
wander into otherworldly glooms of song
rising from earthy depths.

They have no notion of death,
no knowledge of the thing descending
from the heavens
to tear them
                flailing
                        skywards.

They are here
then they are gone: quiver, whisker
                                and tail,
those translucent ears and spindly claws.

Did they dream it, that short life?

Defying Gravity

He turns mice into angels, stalks hoodoo crows
for their blackness and sorcery;
on hot days, scales branches and fences to lie baking

on the asphalt roof, or appears at the window
like a spectre, silent and expectant.
Always expectant, especially when there is chicken.

He is everywhere: gunning from hedges to scatter
his shadows in castle ruins, or bombing the paths of dogs
in a race to the trees.

See him defying gravity: bins and roofs and fence posts,
cannoning into the dark below cars
or through hedgerows.

He owns these streets, patrols the far perimeters
seeking out the opposition, giving them dead eyes
and rolling on by with his Brando swagger.

Mornings, I find him curled by the oven dreaming,
a tremble of heartbeat on his tongue, the collapse in his jaws
of some brief quivering life, all feathers and spirit.

He unwinds to greet me, lies belly up, soft paws folding
and unfolding, those incredible green eyes parting to fix me,
his needle-claws holding me light as a bird's.

Starlings

We use folders of bamboo and deerbone
to construct you: slinted claw
and oilbead plumage, its gloss-speckle and lustre

crisp-folded on the cusp of winter.
Tweezers pin your reedy legs
and thorny beaks, wings blown

from mountain folds and pleats,
their feather-strata paper-cut-sharp
and glorious as angels'.

Evenings, we line you up in trees to roost,
wind you up to hear your clockwork grobbling
and deep space radio whirrs.

Each dawn, exhilarated by the light,
you sing in clicks and shrills, wolf-whistles
and bright cellophane twists,

then fly your squadron down to land
and dandle determinedly across the grass
to yesterday's pecked apples.

Fieldfares descend in reverse folds.
Unfazed you dance defence,
flyweight boxers on your thinstalk legs.

In dreams, we gather you in, gently open out
and press flat your mulberry squares,
their iridescent foil,

store you in a drawer, loose-wrapped
in leaves of tissue, for emergencies:
secret trapdoors to another life,

fast and dark and beautiful.

Badger

The front end of a badger
has halted in its crawl
towards the verge,
spilt bag of rotted fruits,
bittersweet, hypericum;

his carpety fur
someone needs to fold
and hem
before the crows come
stealing beakfuls of tat.

Gone the big grey stroll
and swagger;
in planetary wilderness
he wanders, trawling
scattered light for meaning.

There is grit in his fur,
past worlds in his bones,
earth-smell, sweet and cold
of slug and snail

carrying him deeper
and deeper away from
the roar of lights, the black
shriek that felled him.

By evening, someone
with a shovel moves him,
slings him off
into the hedge

and there he rests,
reluctant warrior,
teeth bared through leaves
of bryony and sorrel,

his fixed eye watching
for worm and grub
and beetle, burrowing up
to claim him.

Fox Map

Over time
you become landscape:

something sinking away
to create valleys and lowlands.

I imagine a clear stream
descending in troughs
and eddies

resisted by your fur
     to pool
  in brilliant
hemispheres.

Your eye,
clear as glass, green/gold of sorrel
or birch, backlit and evening
is gone
   – sewn in
     – blind:
a scar on a long hill.

Over time
you become stranger:
paths peter out, lost
in contours raised by bone,

a quiet tectonic shift
redefining earth,

the stone and soil
   and frost
that built you.

Owl feather, Richard's Castle

It was a moment balanced on a hilltop,
a snapshot sun lighting Richard's Castle:
goats perched on ruined walls,

primroses dappling the straggled grass
and Wales rolling untidily
all the way to the livid line of the horizon.

It was a kestrel moment,
a pause in the buffets of wind as the sun broke out
and shadows blew away like crows

when you spoke of possibilities,
of days we could wander our grassy tumbled turret
with no going back.

I reached down, picked up a feather snagged
upon a twig, smoothed its barbs,
and the day carried on.

Last breath

Drawing the field-edge to a knot,
scanning windward sweeps of scrub,
eye-gold splashed from ferric pools,
she is the buffeted grass,
a demon crow, a sudden curl of smoke
tearing lungs of field mice,
their redcurrant hearts.

Lost amongst paths of vanished towns,
desolate farms, rusting tractors,
she wanders every breath of wind,
a question mark at beech and blackthorn,
her heart a perfect damson,
galls rooted in the tissue
of her belly.

She allows me her full weight
only with the last breath.
The violet oil of absence fogs her eyes
and she is gone.
Still we expect her soft tread
over wet grass, stone path,
cold tiles.

Milk

It's all still here: seascapes of celandine
and clover, trampled earth pooling bitter water,
tremors of shirred light where she stood
scattered and silent

and, way above, a pair of buzzards arcing
and mewling, whirligig larks and their wheedling,
the whole earth and sky swimming in motes
flung from wing and lung, notes carried on the air
seams on a perfect cranium.

Remember her small, determined fingers
working the needle, the mesmerising thimble,
those boxes of patterns and buttons, bundles
of bright silks to be arranged in rows, to be left
perfectly wound.

Below the oak, cows still sense cloud,
never raise their oilbloom eyes to the cumulus;
bright as algae the spume of cud in their mouths,
those lunging tongues quick as eels.

Dawn and dusk, still they carry their awkward frames
to the clunk and swish of the shed,
the warm milk chugging through an octopus of pipes.

Oblivious to the passing of time longer than day or storm,
they cross the land below the church where once
a dairyman, once a husband, curls in the ground,
ribs unbound, tongue shrunk to a starling's.

Remember him leaning to bang his pipe on the hearth,
flickering in matchlight as he sat back
sucking the flame into a hot glow,
his magician's smoke billowing into the room.

She does not go there.
Nowadays we find her in the kitchen,
slicing the loaf, sliding the bread under the grill,
yoghurt spooned in dishes and a bowl of syrup
cooling on the sill.

Outside the house, the blinkered horse stands
like a ghost, with his cart,
stands like a ghost till his skin grows translucent
and his bones smoulder with phosphorus.

It's all still here:
the lights are on in Number 36 and breakfast laid,
the milk poured, waiting.

Fieldfares

They steal away sunlight on belly and wing,
each stipple and streak, each blade-edge
tilted to the wind.

Below their squabbling, their barrelling
tin-scrape scolding, the determined unpicking
of this low grey sky,
        we trace a line back to silence,
in its lee, find a portal to another time:
a holloway to copse and clearing, leaf
and riotous winding weed,
                an eternity of green,
a pool where you can lie and dream
among the curious flickering fry.

There is a path, but camouflaged:
                        an old way,
trodden by the ghosts of sheep,
hidden in the rain lingering on twigs,
                their mystical upside world.

Only your mind can steal into this world;
your bones, your terrible human heart,
you must leave behind.

Pike Nest

He died just here,
surging skywards in belts of riverspray
      to land snagged
between unexpected limbs,

his final minutes gusting a leaf storm
– that whipcrack bucking and twisting –
bark rasping his skin.

Now, blind and perished,
jaws snapped wide as if for air,
      he hangs.

Small birds venture in, inspect
the airy tomb,
its scattered gallery of light on bone,

lay their young, pulse and flutter
in a nest of grass and hair upon
his shrivel-tongue.

Next spring, we'll find its shredded silks,
seams split, birds flown,
      mossy contents thrown
onto the riverbank below.

Zander

two miles on, it slows,
flows darkly below roach poles,
dripping cresses

they sling the zander in hedges
snapping the air
leaf litter crusting their cold skins
tinshine eyes coated with dust

gutting, later, I feel no remorse
slitting abdomen from chest to tail
pulling free the soft roe

this one a baby
such a tiny ribcage
bones thin as hair

the kitchen fills with steam
a must of simmering potatoes
outside, in the dark, rain falls
thick as glass

Equivocal

Light spills both ways:
silhouetting stands of blackthorn on the lane

and climbing the slow hill, striping the turf, its grey horse
racing a big sky.

Along the line of the fence, a ghost owl flies on silent wing
while the weasel creeps to her nest.

The weasel creeps to her nest without brushing a leaf
breathing its pinbone mess of pellet and fur.

Darkling beetles steady at rustle and hiss, wait
for the long yolk falling.

Along the line of the fence, the ghost owl flies to her nest,
early light tracing the edge of her wing in each direction.

Her ears pinpoint sound in delay; last night's start
and patter, her hunger, buried in the fall of rain.

She disappears from sight, leaving her silence
and a glimmer of wire.

In the hedge, something woven from air and tats of down
is staring, its flyblown carcass stirring as if waking.

Earth resumes its humming; celandine secures the verge.
On the hill, the horse stoops to graze.

Linnets

It catches us unaware:
the broken sky blown blue,
the last of the contrails, the last
of our days.
        We watch the light
spilling down cracks in the long hill,
cracks in the long hours.

Dragged from the kindness of sleep,
radio news drowning the strange silence,
we mourn our secret landscapes,
the people we felt we knew
        but will never meet again:
our ghost worlds
and the ghost spring sliding away,
stealing with it our lives.

Each day, we walk the old paths,
try to find our way back.
The elder's in leaf, blackthorn starry
with blossom.
No one speaks but
        there is still song.
Finch and thrush and wren

        and flurries of linnets
                sweeping the sky
untying the breeze with their calls,
questioning the tilt of the earth
                and the shifting hill,
its trees and paths shuddering
with light.

Vixen

and there
through this Japanese ghost garden
this monochrome dreamscape
slips a half-dreamt wraith

born from the last shades of dusk
she is tip tip toeing on footfall so soft
it uncurls snails
dizzies galaxies in dew

her vagabond heart
beats with the tremors of the earth
balances on owl call
and the breeze rushing the trees

behind her swim timorous worlds
we can never enter

so slight and swift she moves
that without the moon billowing through
the cherry and all the fallen blossom
luminous as snow
I would not see her

I am wren

Beyond the walls, the song of linnets
– syllables of evening light
and the translucent green of sharp fruits –
doodles its strange calligraphy
of query
        and reply.

In my quiet world
I have no more how or when
or why.
Already they are growing, my wings.
I feel the jut of feathers,
a honeycomb of bones lighter than air,
the rasp of vanes emerging.

I wished to be goldfinch
with its strong beak and bright boho colours
(that unwinding whimsy of song)
but I shall be wren, brown as twigs,
a feathered cocoon pulsing
                with life and attitude,
here and here and there,
        eye and beak and gone.

Beyond the damp dark earth
is sky
and I am soon to be this tiny bird;
built of the thinnest bone,
I am almost flying.

Kestrel

wired to weave perfect light
       wind-buffeted
winnowing ocean-air turbulence

pharaoh-eyed indigo-deep
resting momentarily
       in dark-path leaf-curl
scent-seeking
       nightjar-crouch

then
       eye strike
shadow-patter grass-spire quiver

cryptic tilting
       dipping
sudden tunnel-thrust   and
       lift
lift
       adjust
accommodate the crosswind
hover
       hold
         hold
hold

my beautiful kohl-eyed
tempest angel

Made certain by the signs of birds

A kingdom made certain by the signs of birds:
columns of air and leaves born from pearled seed,
here and here and there, eye and beak and gone;
sky breaking through the canopy,
a backwash of blue light.

It's bigger than angels, this updraught of life,
each burst of leaf, each hum of wing and song spilling
like beads of air, the rush of a flatstone creek,
its bellyrock slide and sparkle,
that backwash of blue light.

There are shadows, of course, and dead things:
the chewed stalks of wings, mud-trodden
carcasses of ideas, lost paths through dead trees,
but always the signs of birds
and that backwash of blue light.

Indigo Dreams Publishing Ltd
24, Forest Houses
Cookworthy Moor
Halwill
Beaworthy
Devon
EX21 5UU
www.indigodreams.co.uk